HIDING IN
WETLANDS

Deborah Underwood

www.raintreepublishers.co.uk
Visit our website to find out
more information about
Raintree books.

To order:
☎ Phone 0845 6044371
🖹 Fax +44 (0) 1865 312263
🖳 Email myorders@raintreepublishers.co.uk

Customers from outside the UK please telephone +44 1865 312262

Raintree is an imprint of Capstone Global Library Limited,
a company incorporated in England and Wales having
its registered office at 7 Pilgrim Street, London, EC4V 6LB
– Registered company number: 6695582

Edited by Rebecca Rissman and Nancy Dickmann
Designed by Joanna Hinton Malivoire
Picture research by Tracy Cummins
Originated by Capstone Global Library
Printed and bound in China by Leo Paper Products Ltd.

ISBN 978 0 431 01316 9
15 14 13 12 11
10 9 8 7 6 5 4 3 2 1

British Library Cataloguing in Publication Data
Underwood, Deborah.
  Hiding in wetlands. -- (Creature camouflage)
  1. Wetland animals--Juvenile literature. 2. Camouflage
(Biology)--Juvenile literature.
  I. Title II. Series
  591.4'72-dc22

Acknowledgements
We would like to thank the following for permission to
reproduce photographs: Corbis p. 9 (© Tony Arruza); FLPA
pp. 13, 14, 17, 18 (© David Hosking), 23, 24 (© S & D & K
Maslowski); Getty Images pp. 27 (Elliott Neep), 28 (James
Randklev); Minden Pictures pp. 11, 12 (© Flip De Nooyer),
21, 22 (© Jan Van Arkel); naturepl.com pp. 6 (© David
Kjaer), 10 (© Steve Knell), 19, 20 (© Barrie Britton), 25, 26
(© Rolf Nussbaumer); Photolibrary p. 7 (Paul Thompson);
Shutterstock pp. 4 (© Kevin M. Kerfoot), 5 (© Mike Pluth),
8 (© Luca Bertolli), 15, 16 (© Angelina Dimitrova), 29
(© Pavol Kmeto).

Cover photograph of an American bittern (Botaurus
lentiginosus) reproduced with permission of Visuals
Unlimited, Inc. (© Joe McDonald).

We would like to thank Michael Bright for his invaluable help
in the preparation of this book.

Every effort has been made to contact copyright holders of
any material reproduced in this book. Any omissions will
be rectified in subsequent printings if notice is given to
the publisher.

All the Internet addresses (URLs) given in this book were
valid at the time of going to press. However, due to the
dynamic nature of the Internet, some addresses may have
changed, or sites may have changed or ceased to exist
since publication. While the author and publisher regret any
inconvenience this may cause readers, no responsibility for
any such changes can be accepted by either the author or
the publisher.

Contents

Some words are printed in bold, **like this**. You can find out what they mean by looking in the glossary.

What are wetlands like?

A wetland is a place where water covers the ground for some or all of the year. Marshes and swamps are two types of wetlands.

A marsh is a wetland where grasses are the main kind of plant.

The main plants in swamps are trees.

Wetlands can be found along coasts by the sea. They can also be found near rivers, lakes, and ponds.

Living in wetlands

Wetlands are home to many different types of animals. Some animals live in wetlands all the year round. Some animals stop off in wetlands on their way to other places.

Some deer live in wetlands all the year round.

These egrets have long necks and sharp beaks that allow them to hunt fish, frogs, and other small animals.

Wetland animals have special **features** that help them to **survive** in their wet surroundings. These features are called **adaptations**. For example, ducks have webbed feet to help them swim through the water.

What is camouflage?

Camouflage is an **adaptation** that helps animals to hide. The colour of an animal's skin, fur, or feathers may match the things around it.

A river otter's brown fur can help it **blend in** with mud and rocks.

This water moccasin snake's **patterns** act as camouflage.

Animals that eat other animals are called **predators**. Some predators creep up on the animals they hunt. Others wait for animals to pass by. Camouflage helps predators catch food.

Camouflage is especially important for birds that build nests on the ground.

The animals that **predators** eat are called **prey**. **Camouflage** helps prey animals hide. It makes them harder for predators to find.

Find the wetland animals

Bittern

A bittern is a type of bird. Bitterns live among tall water plants called reeds. The bitterns' feathers are light brown with dark spots.

CAMOUFLAGED

Bitterns walk quietly through the water as they look for food. If a **predator** comes near, a bittern points its head up and stands still. The colour of its feathers helps it to hide in the reeds.

REVEALED

Beaver

Beavers have dark fur. Their flat tails are shaped like paddles. Some beavers dig homes in riverbanks near tree roots. Can you see how their fur can help them to hide in mud or roots?

Young beavers are not as strong as adults. Bears and wolves may try to catch and eat them. The beavers' **camouflage** helps them to hide and keep safe.

REVEALED

Marsh frog

Marsh frogs are green with dark spots. They **blend in** with grasses that grow near ponds and streams. Their camouflage helps to hide them from hungry birds and snakes.

Marsh frogs like to **bask** in the sunshine on riverbanks. If a **predator** comes near, the frogs may flatten their bodies. Then they **blend in** with the ground. Or they may plop back into the water!

REVEALED

Alligator

Alligators have a rough, dark skin that acts as **camouflage**. It helps them to blend in when they lie on the shore, or on floating logs. It also helps them to hide as they float in the water.

An alligator sometimes lies very still and waits for **prey**. Other animals don't notice it. When an animal comes to the water's edge, the alligator grabs it.

REVEALED

Canvasback duck

Male canvasback ducks stand out. They have reddish heads and white backs. But the female ducks have better **camouflage**. Why do you think a female bird might need to **blend in**?

A female canvasback duck lays eggs in a floating nest. She builds the nest among water plants. The colour of her feathers **blends in** with the plants. This helps to keep her safe while she sits on her eggs.

REVEALED

Grass snake

Grass snakes have dark green backs with black marks. They hunt birds and mice on land. They hunt frogs and fish in the water. Grass snakes can stay underwater for over half an hour!

Grass snakes' skin helps them to hide. And if a **predator** attacks, they play dead! They stop moving and make a nasty smell. When the predator goes away, they start moving again.

REVEALED

Muskrat

Muskrats sometimes dig homes in riverbanks. Their brown fur helps them to **blend in** with mud. Their fur also traps air. This helps the muskrats to float.

Mink, eagles, and otters like to eat muskrats. If a muskrat sees a **predator**, it may dive into the water. It can stay underwater for up to 20 minutes!

Red-eared slider turtle

A red-eared slider turtle can easily be mistaken for a rock at the bottom of a stream! The colour of the turtle's shell **blends in** with rocks and water ripples.

CAMOUFLAGED

Red-eared slider turtles eat plants and animals. In the daytime, they crawl out of the water. They **bask** in the sunshine to warm their bodies. The turtles' thick shells help protect them from **predators**.

REVEALED

Can you see how this water vole's brown fur helps it hide?

Many wetland animals **blend in** with the water, plants, and mud. Their feathers, fur, or scaly skin help them to hide in their surroundings.

Animals that stand out

Not all wetland animals hide. A flamingo stands out! Flamingos get their bright pink colour from the small, shrimp-like animals that they eat.

Flamingos often stand for a long time on one leg.

Flamingos eat tiny plants and animals that live in the mud.

Some flamingos live where there are few **predators**. They do not need to hide. Others stay safe by standing in large groups. That way they can warn each other of danger.

Glossary

adaptation special feature that helps an animal survive in its surroundings

bask to bask in the sunshine means to sunbathe

blend in matches well with the things around it

camouflage adaptation that helps an animal blend in with its surroundings

feature special part of an animal

pattern shapes and marks on an animal's skin, fur, or feathers

predator animal that eats other animals

prey animal that other animals eat

survive stay alive

Find out more

Books to read

Animals: A Children's Encyclopedia
   (Dorling Kindersley, 2008)

Introducing Habitats: A Wetland Habitat,
   Molly Aloian (Crabtree Publishing, 2006)

Who Lives Here? Wetland Animals,
   Deborah Hodge (Kids Can Press, 2008)

Websites

www.bbc.co.uk/nature/habitats/Flooded_grass-lands_and_savannas
A BBC website where you can watch films and find out more about your favourite wetland animals.

www.enchantedlearning.com/biomes/swamp/swamp.shtml
Learn more about wetland habitats and the animals who live there.

Index

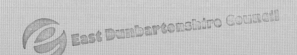